The Renaissance Masters

grayscale coloring book

curated by

Tabz Jones

The Renaissance emerged in Italy in the late 14th century and
reached its height in the late 15th and early 16th centuries.
The period gifted the world some of the most talented and famous
artists in all
of modern history.
This coloring book contains twenty five of my favorite art works
from the era. The grand masters who's work you
will find here are:
Antonio da Correggio
Lucas Cranach the Elder
Albrecht Dürer
Hans Holbein the Elder
Leonardo da Vinci
Michelangelo
Pietro Perugino
Titian
Raphael

I invite you to visit your local museums and search the internet
to find out more about these artists.
This book is volume 2 in The Masters series of coloring books.
You can find the other volumes at most major online retailers or ask your local book
store to carry them!

Tabz Jones
POBox 2137
Alma, AR 72921
www.gothictoggs.net

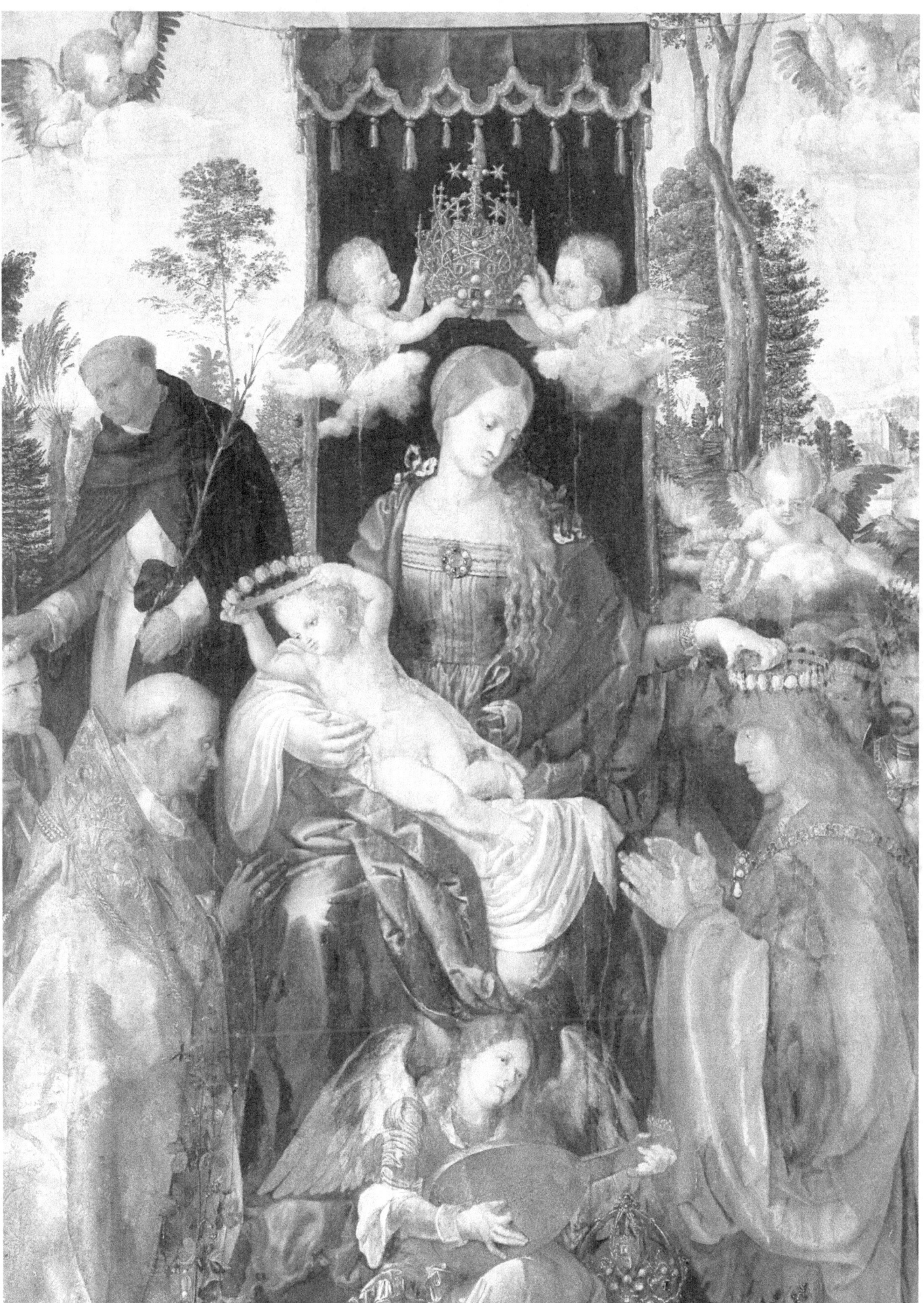

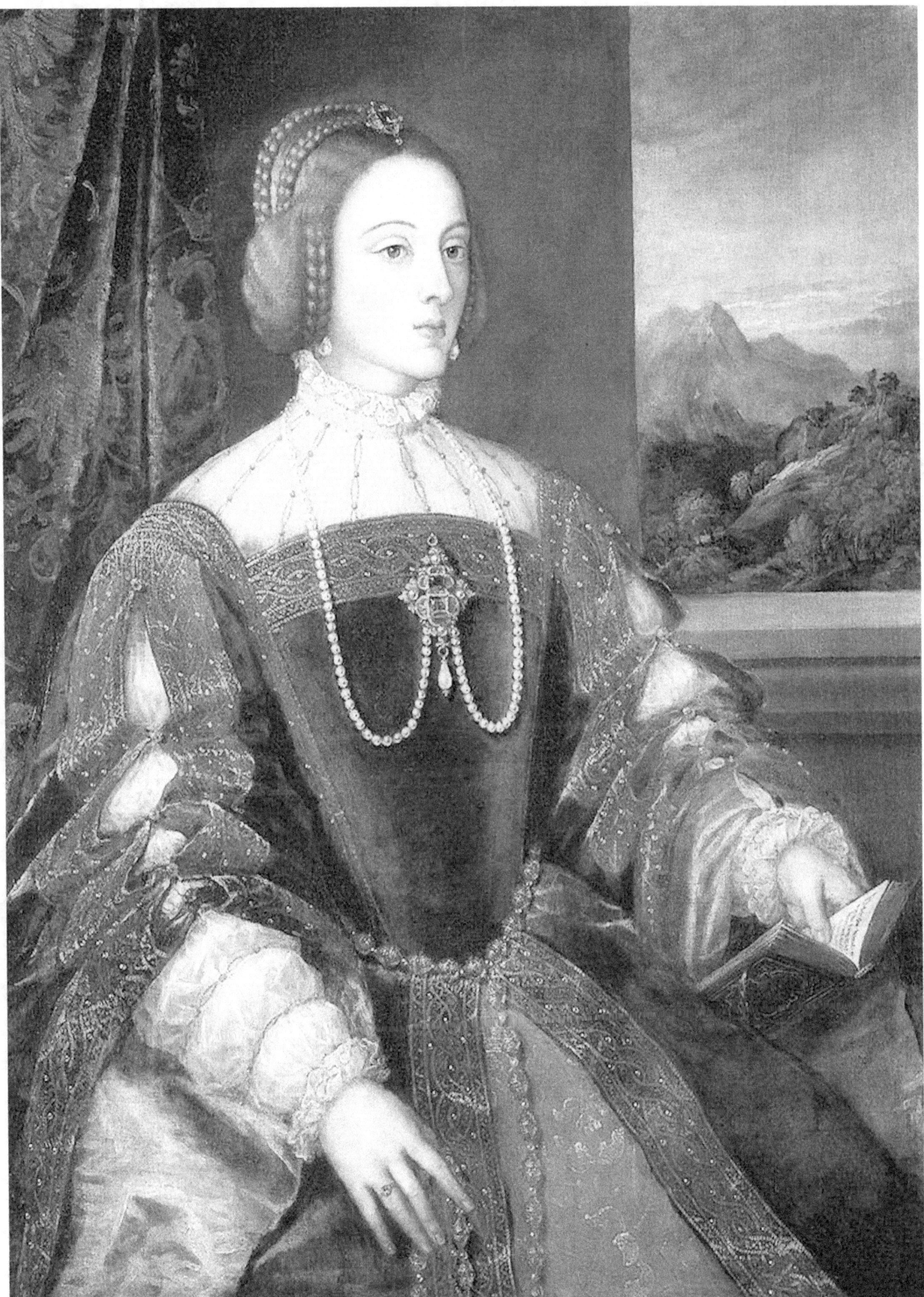

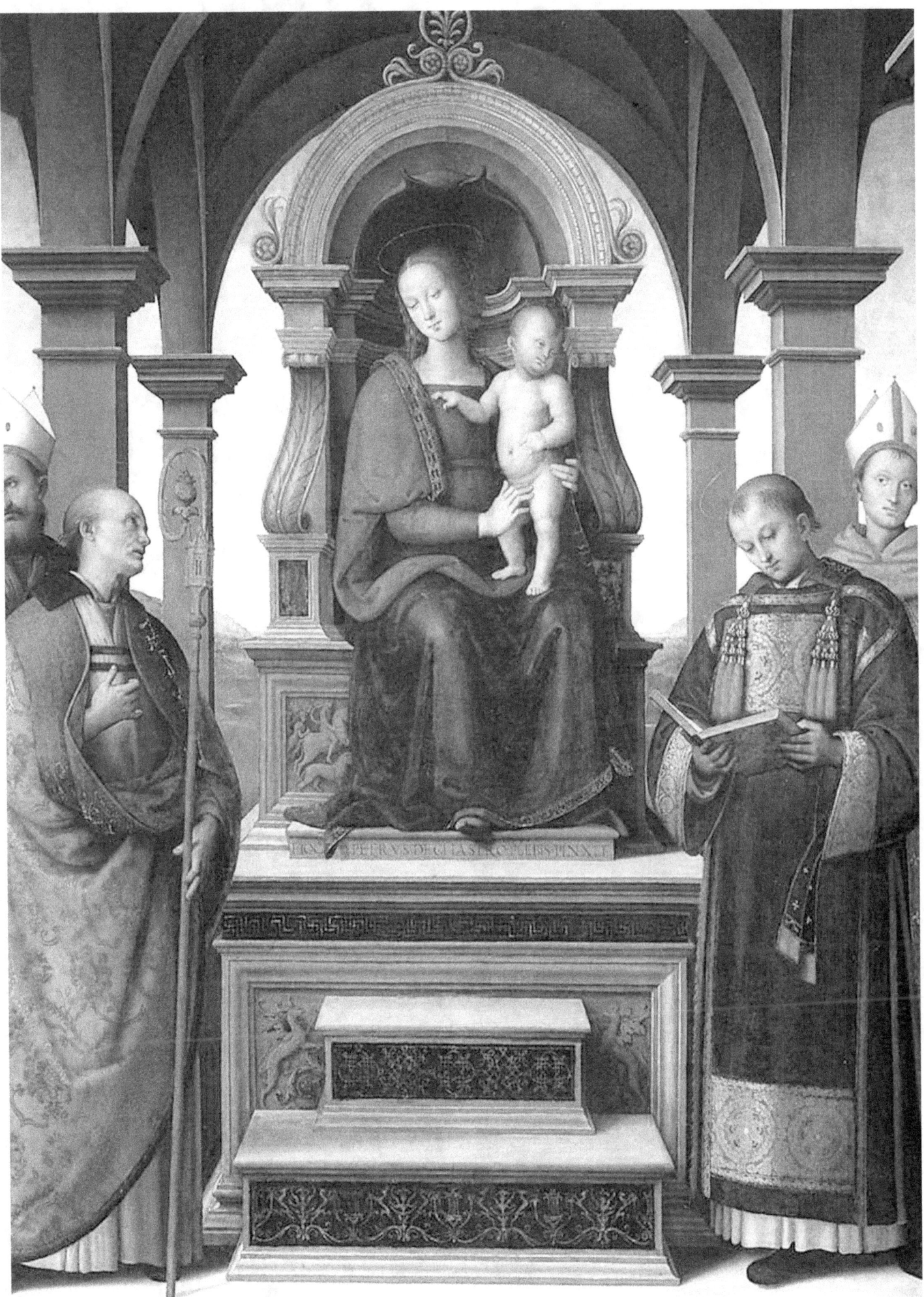

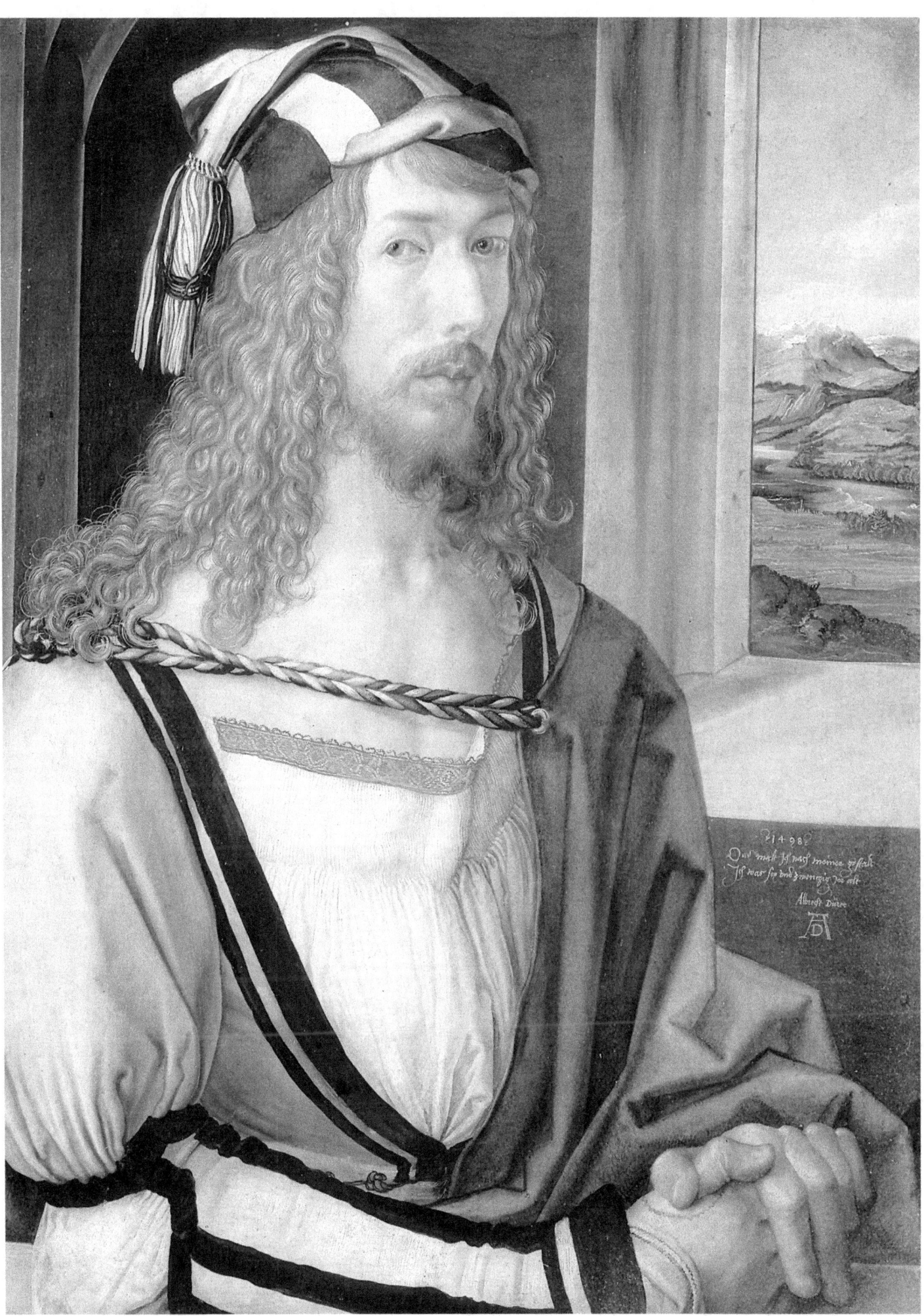

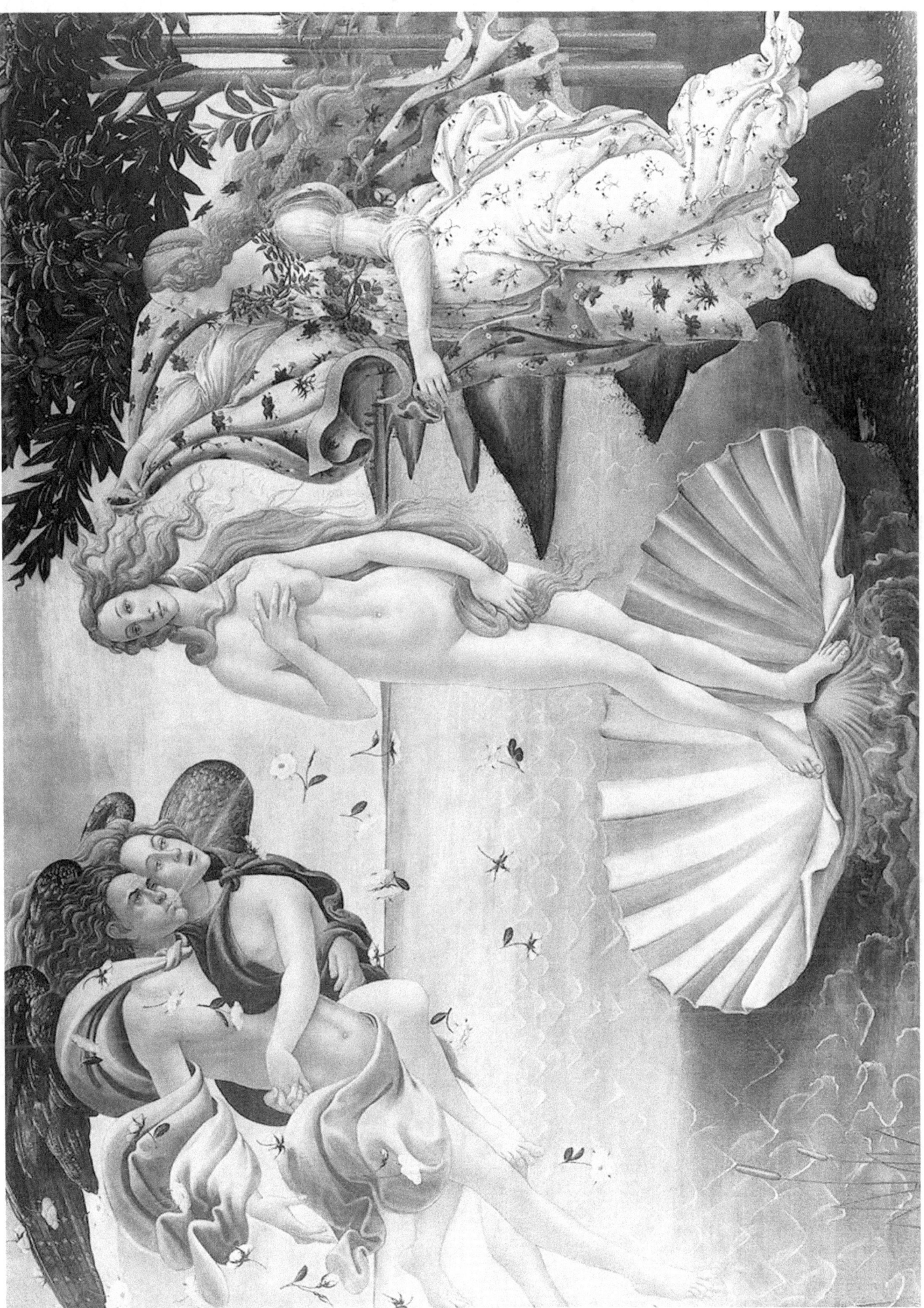

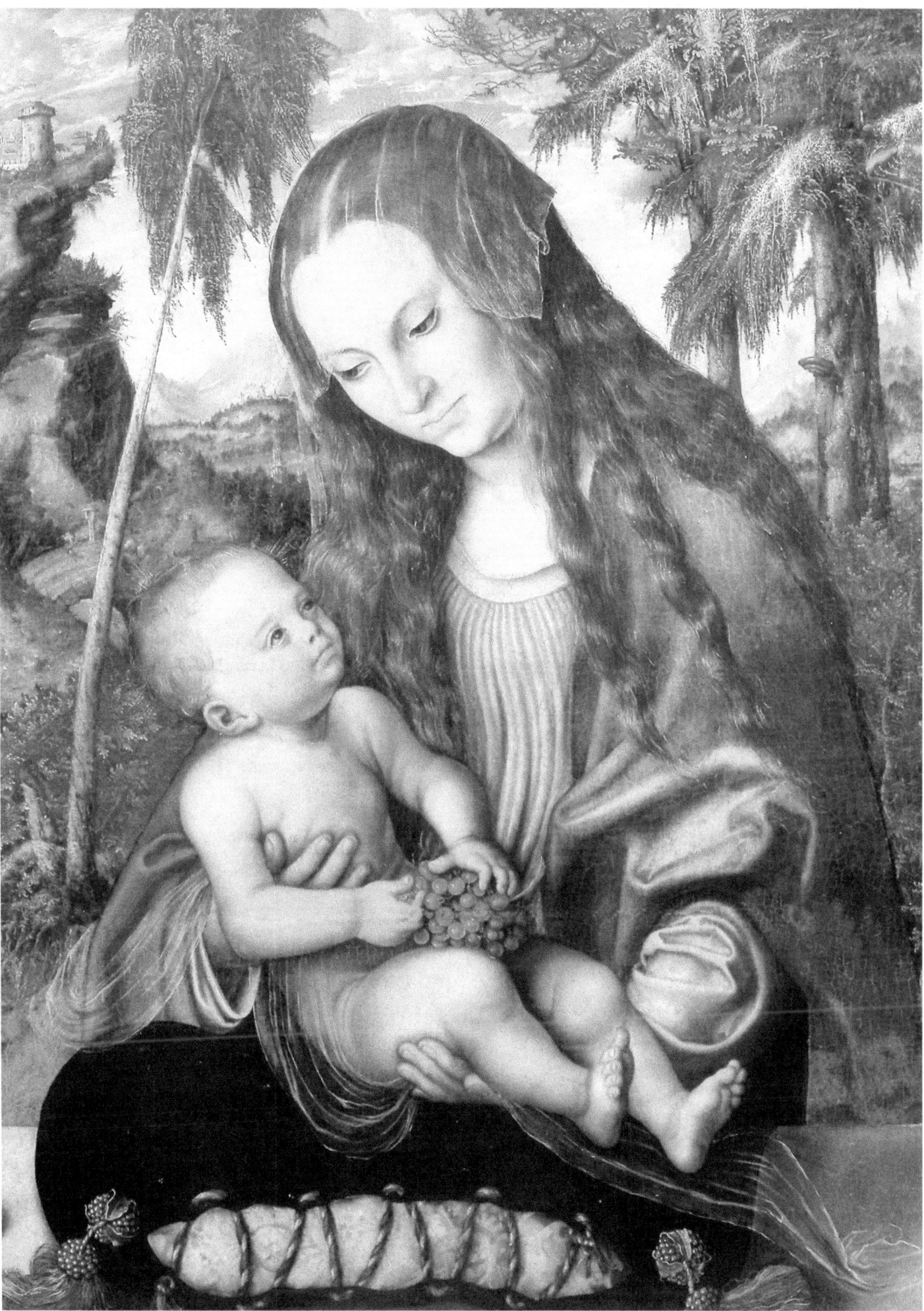

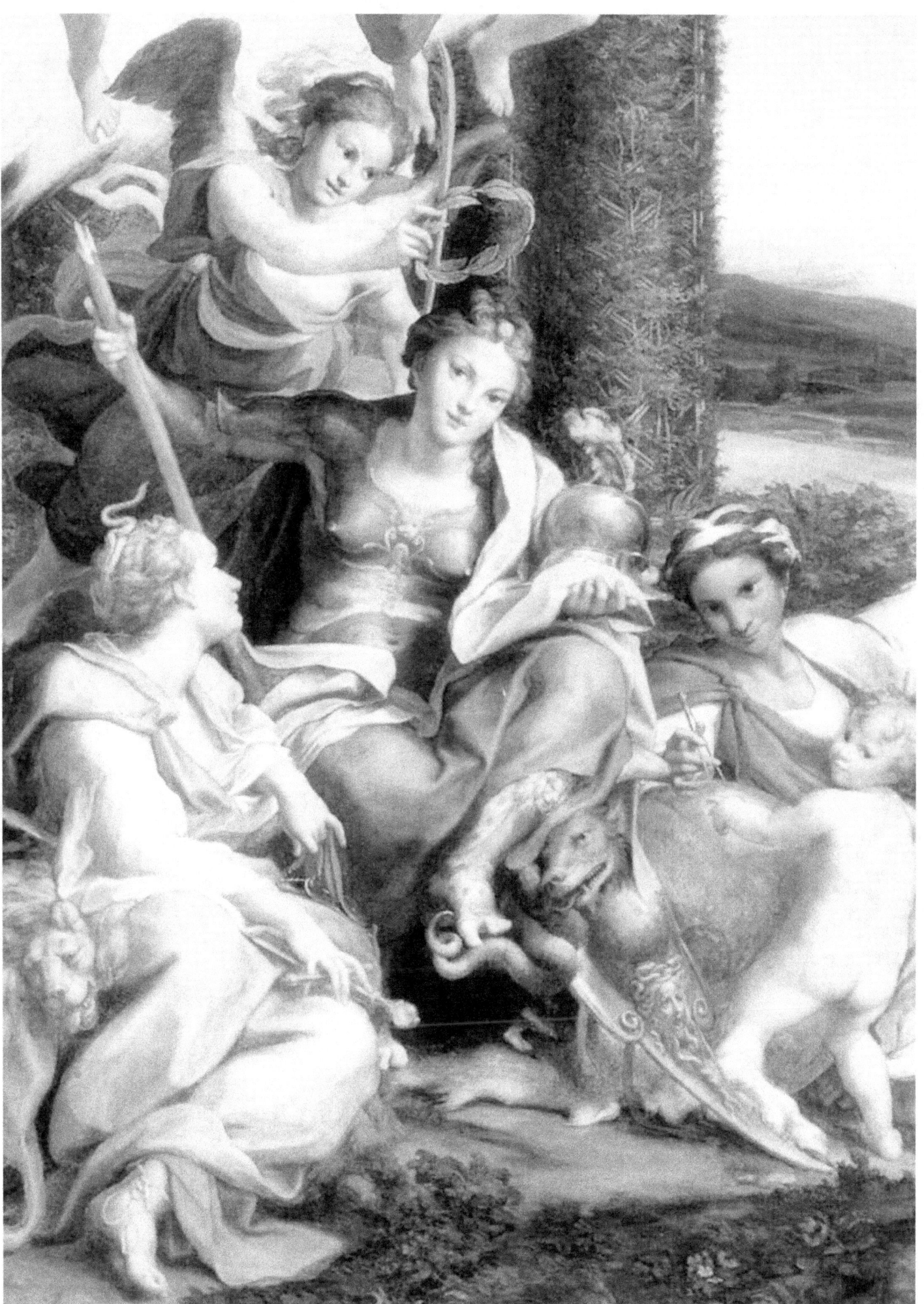

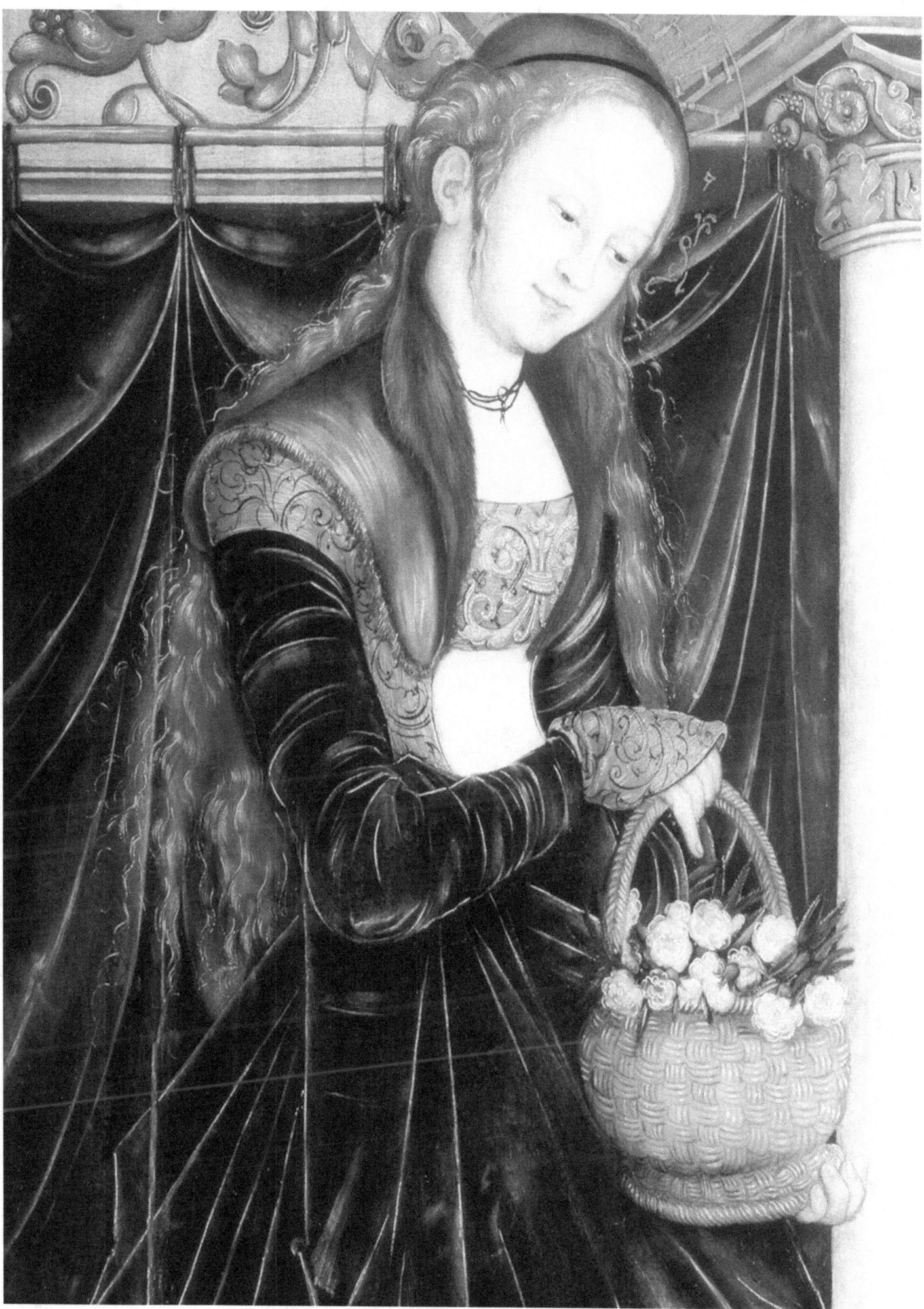

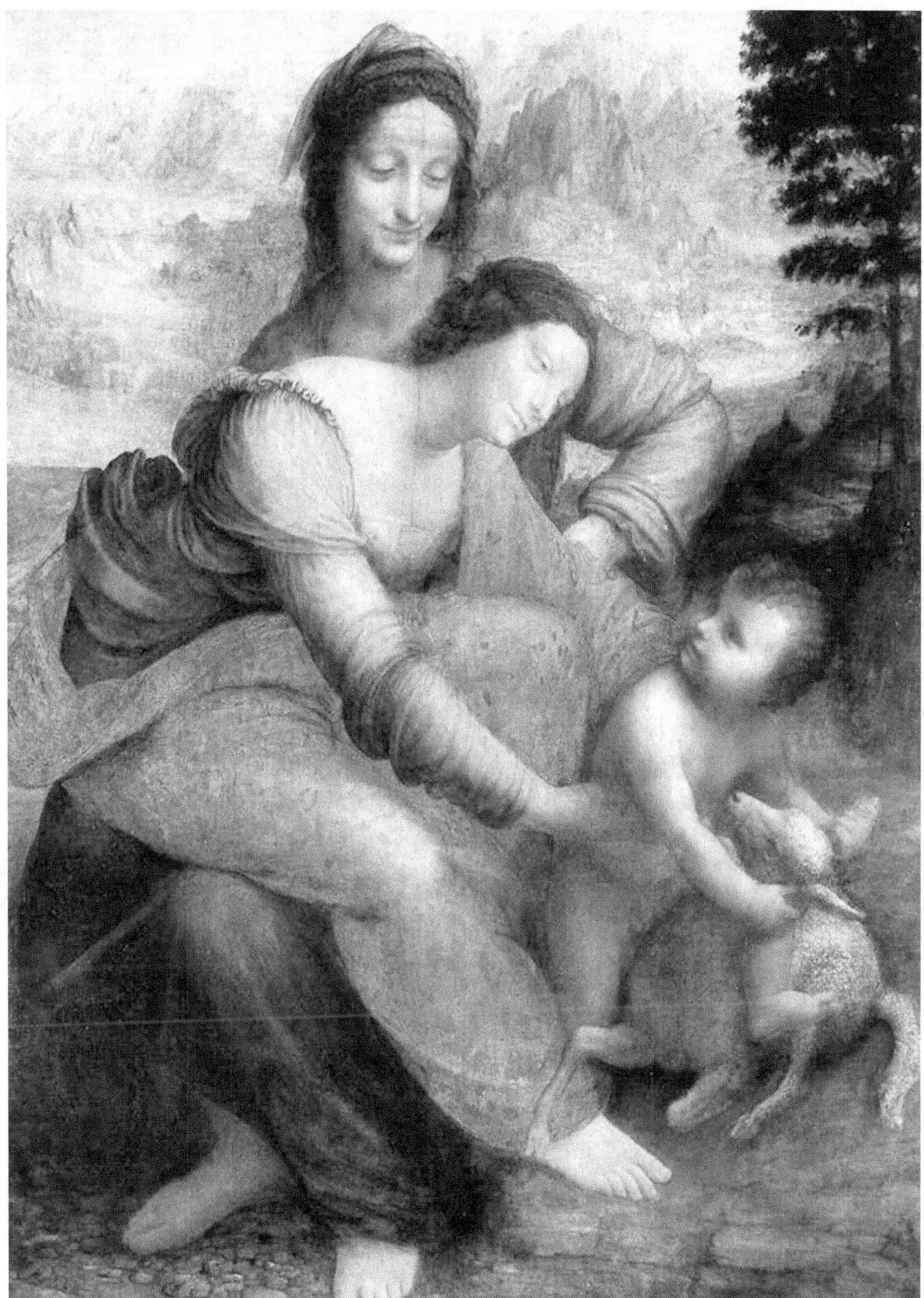

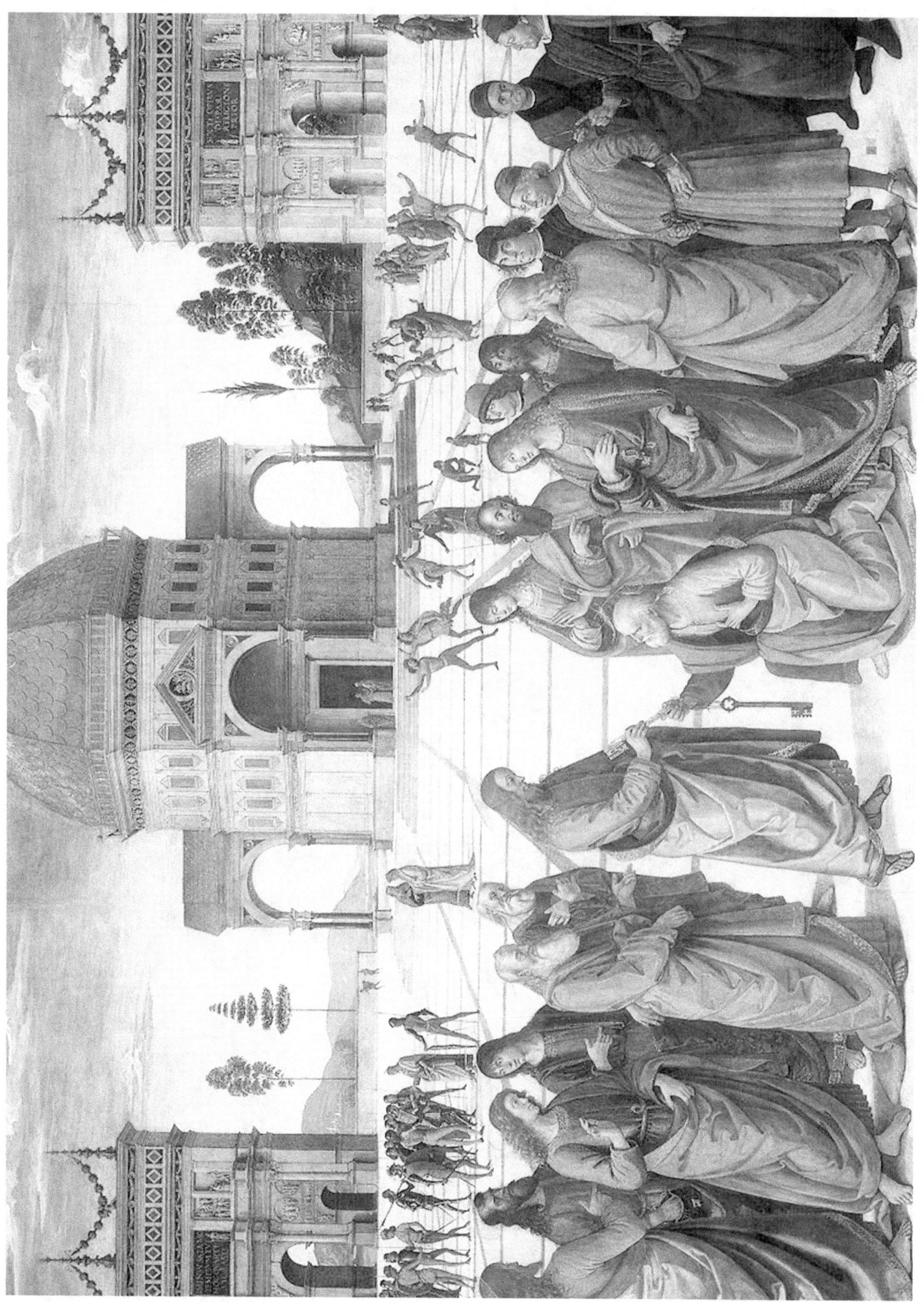

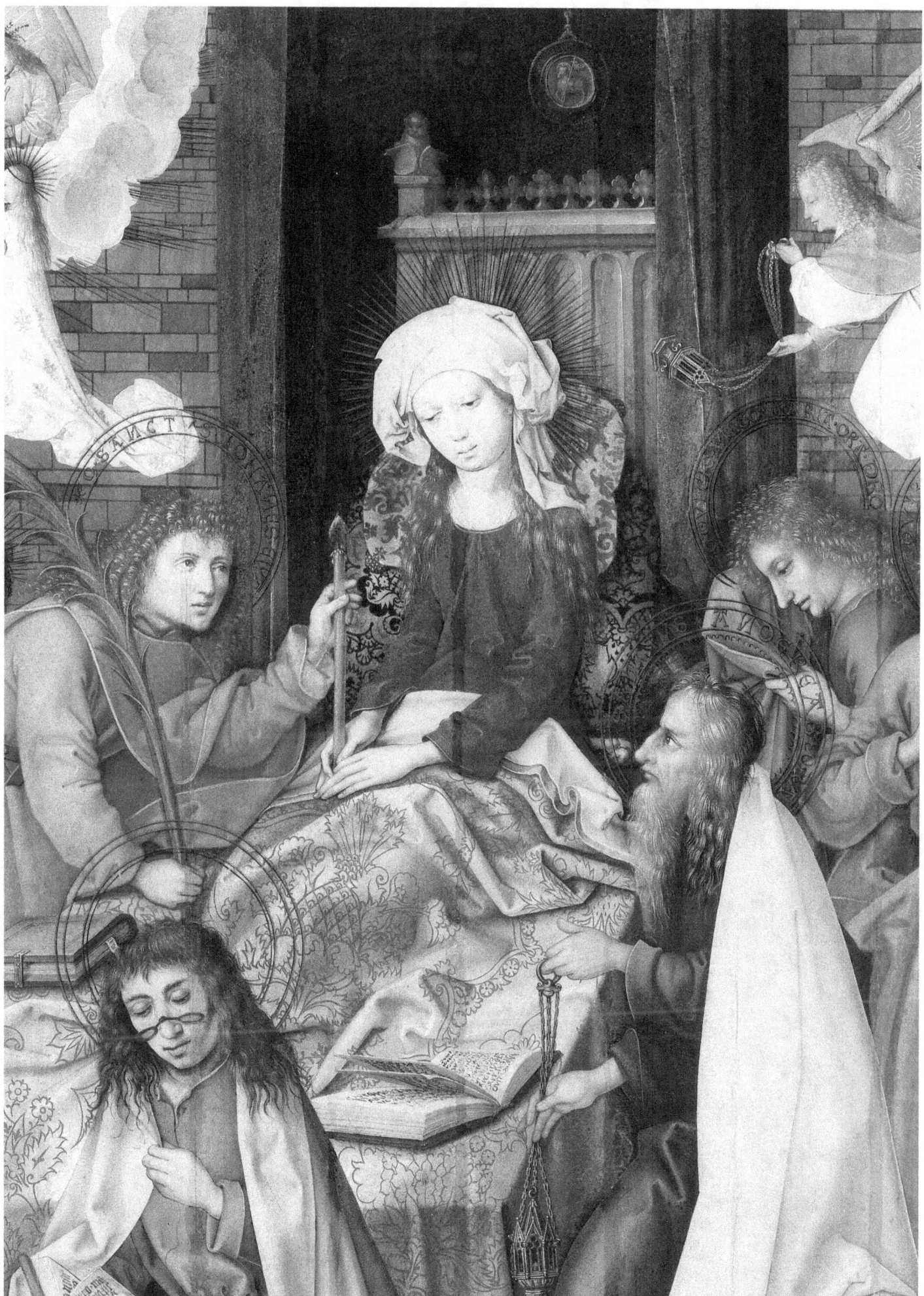

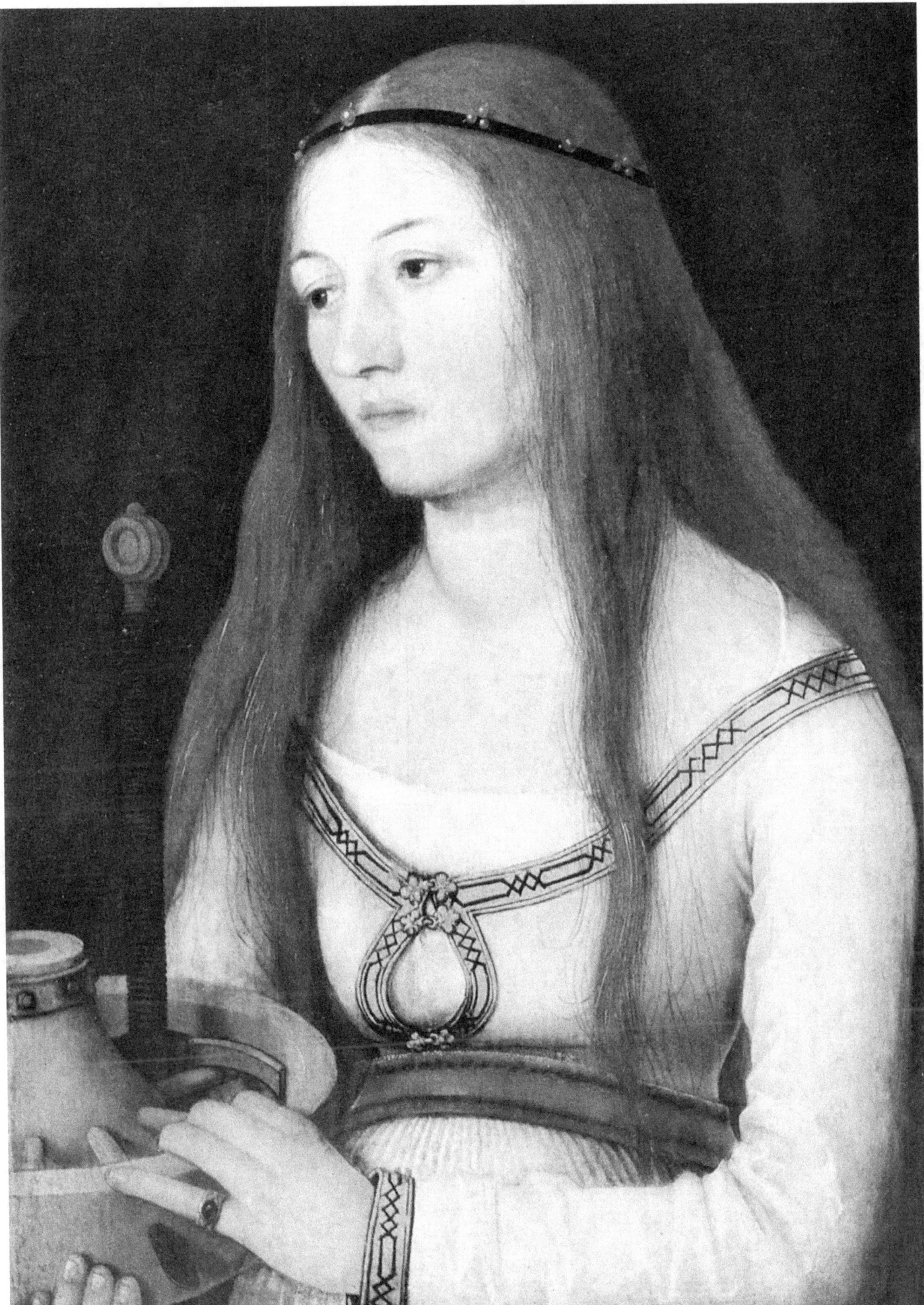

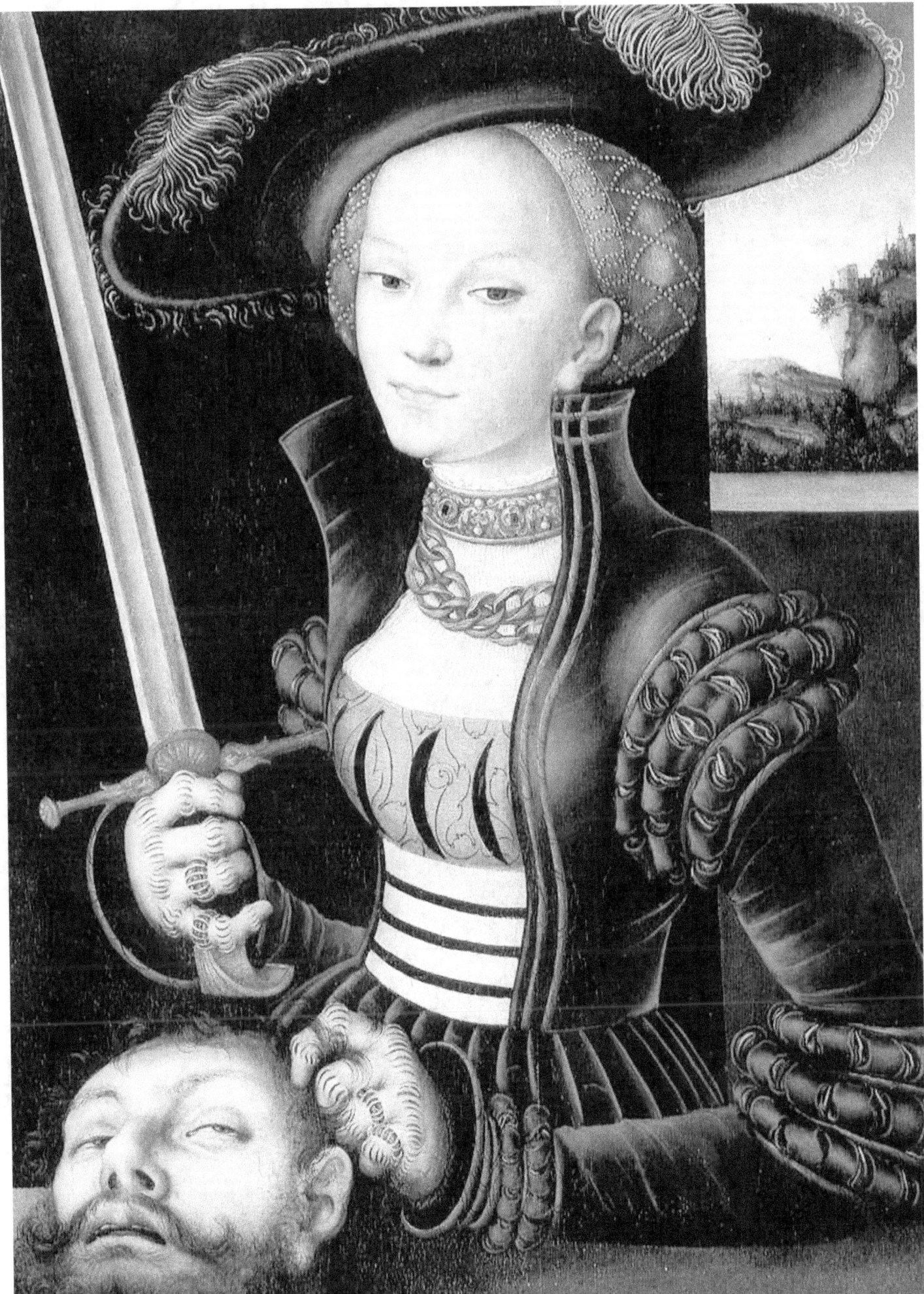

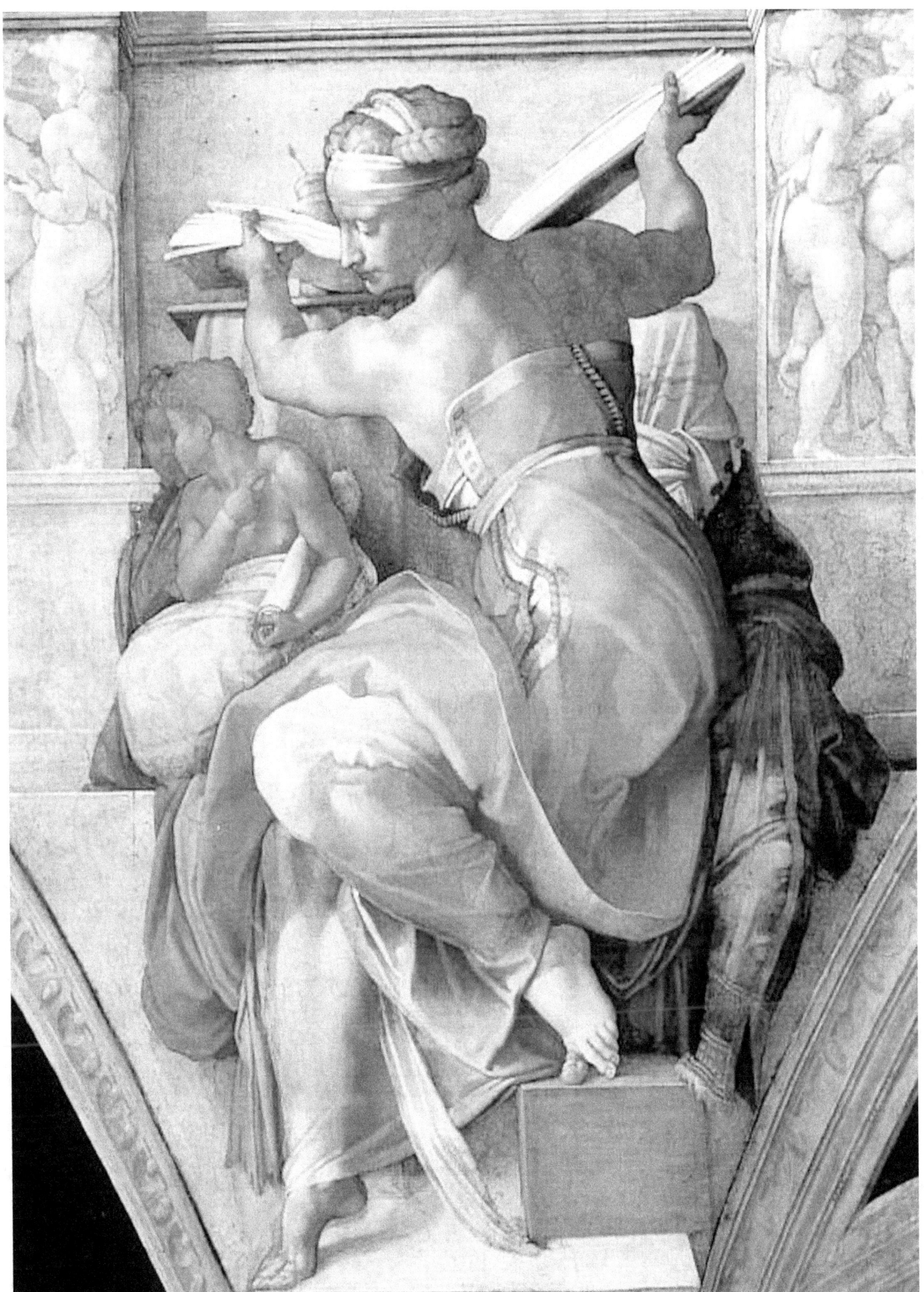

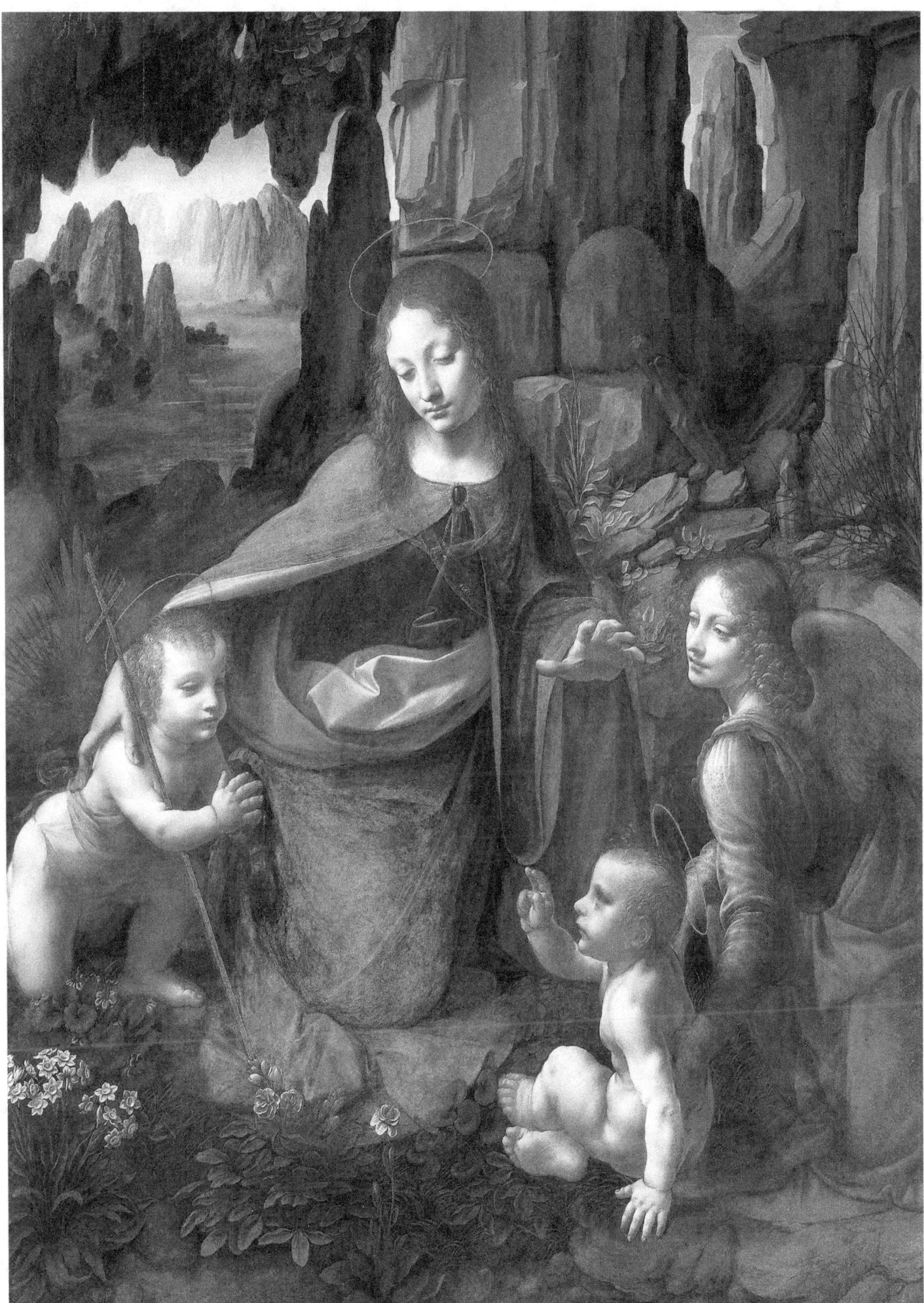

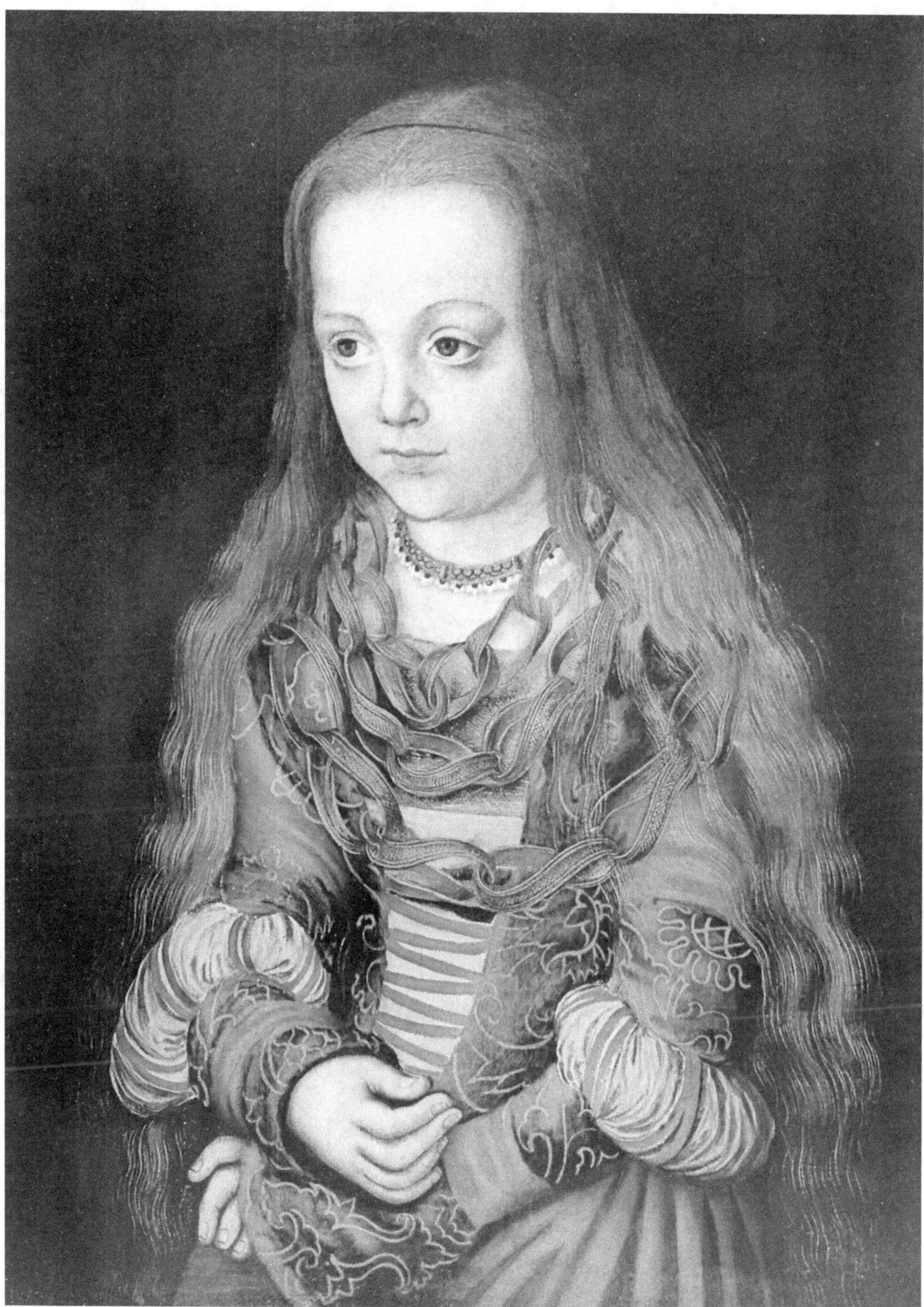

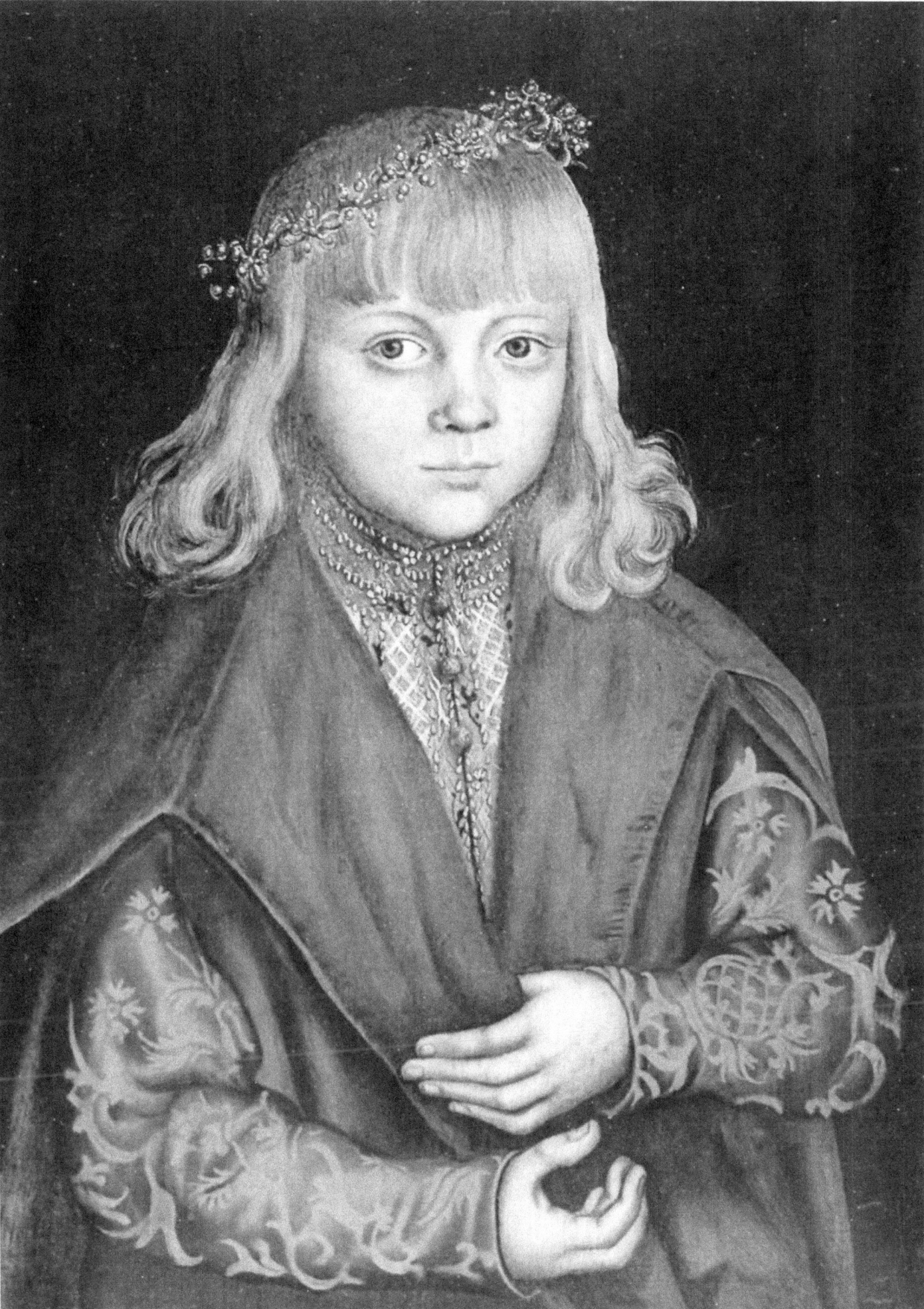

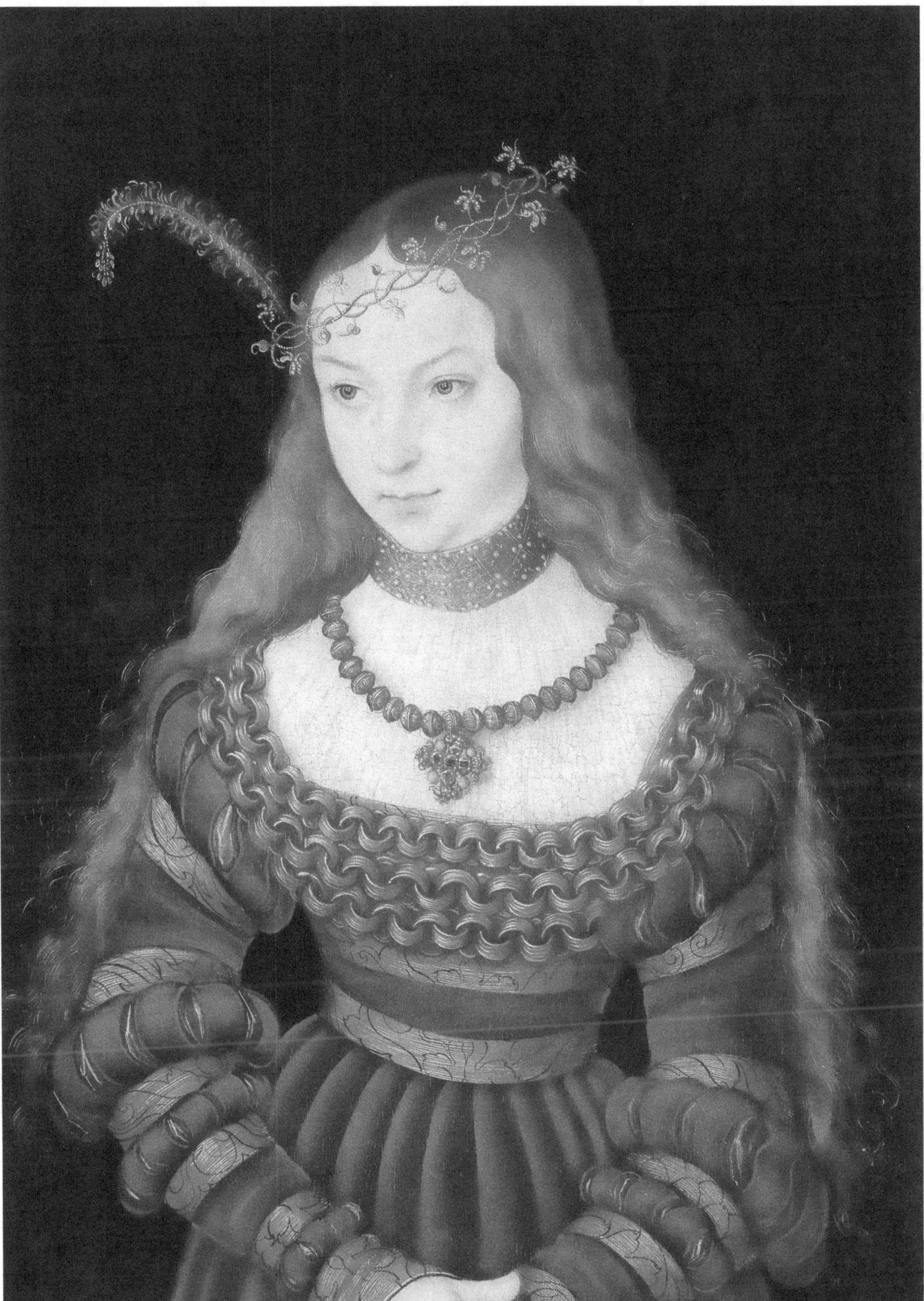

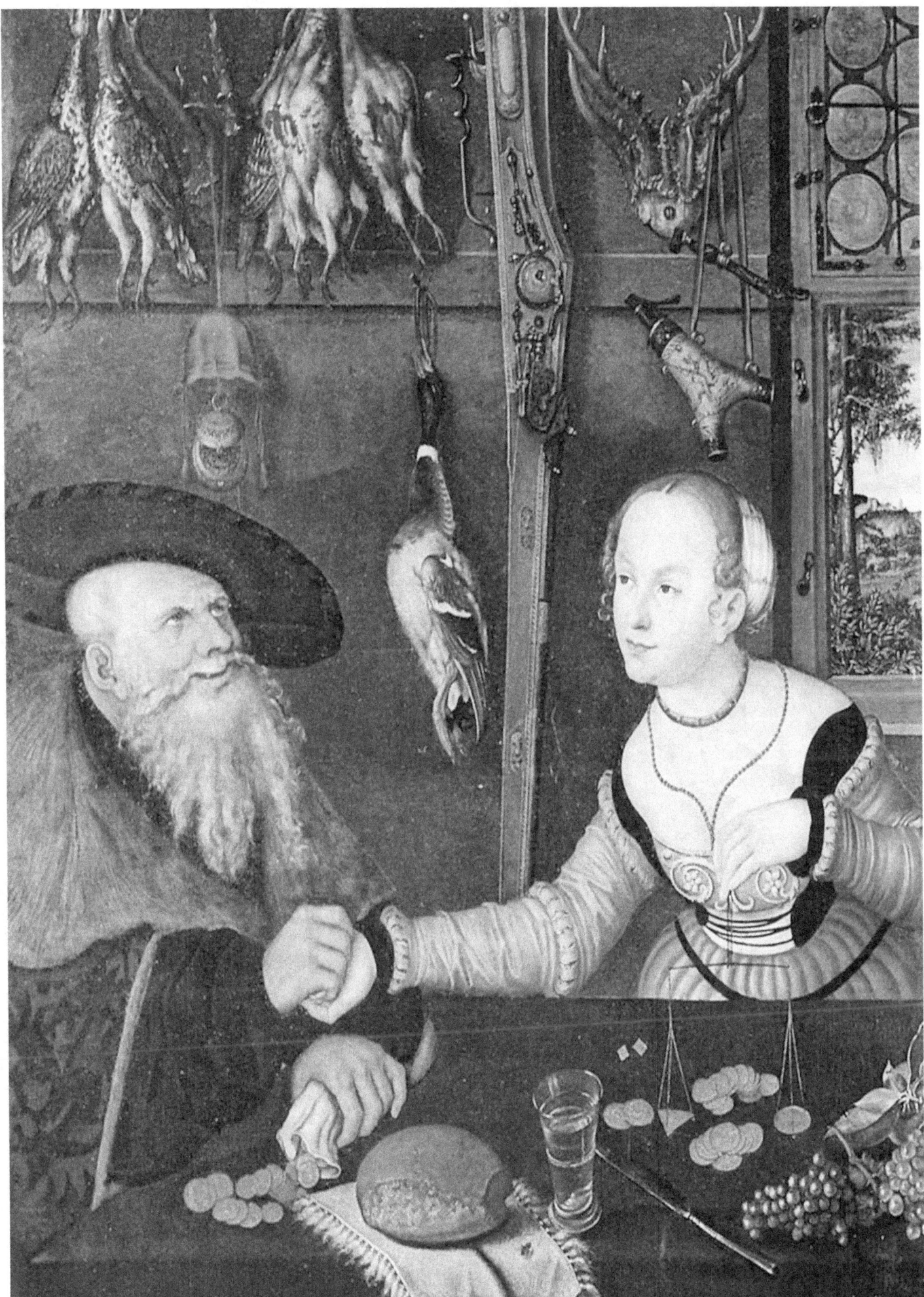

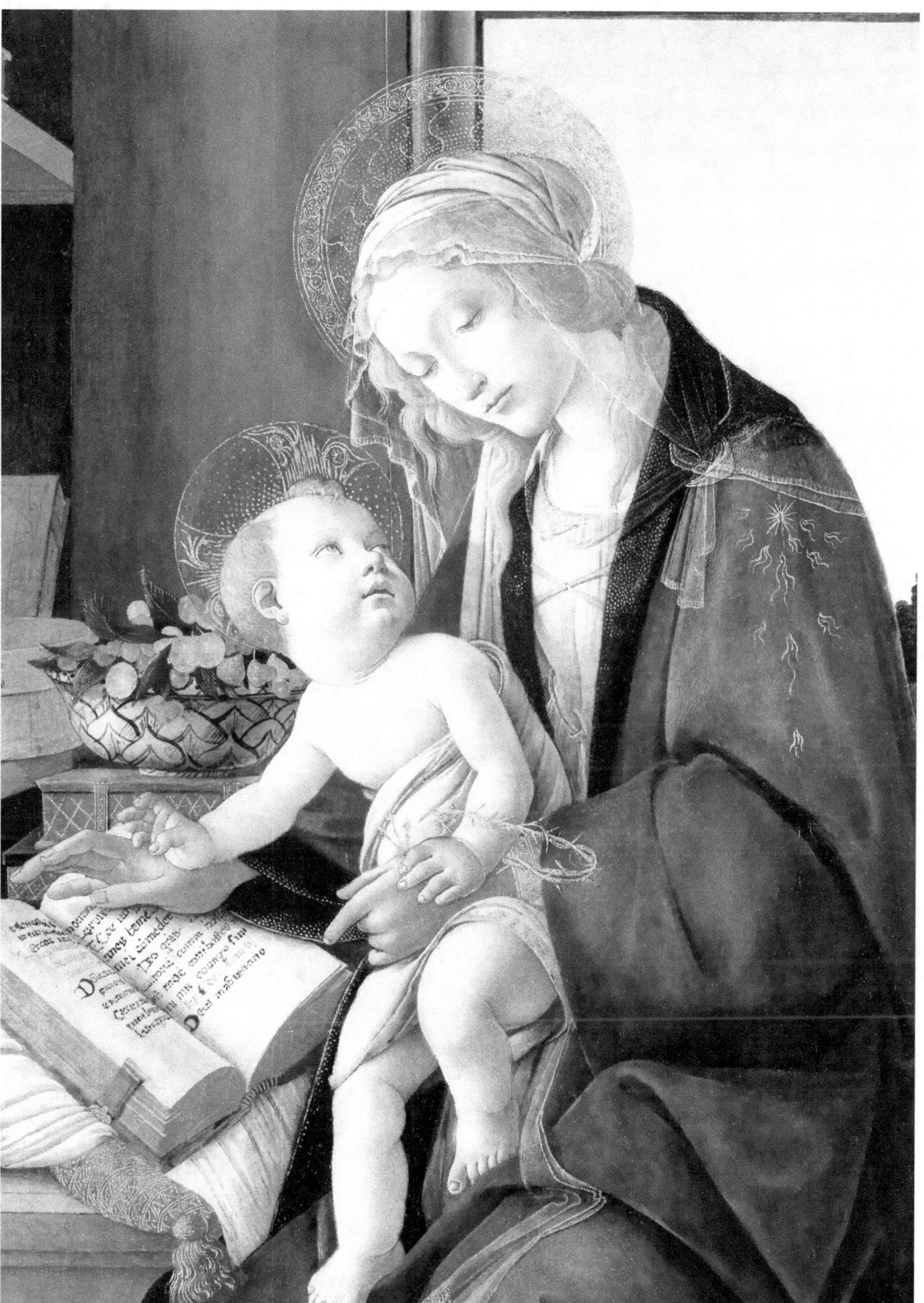

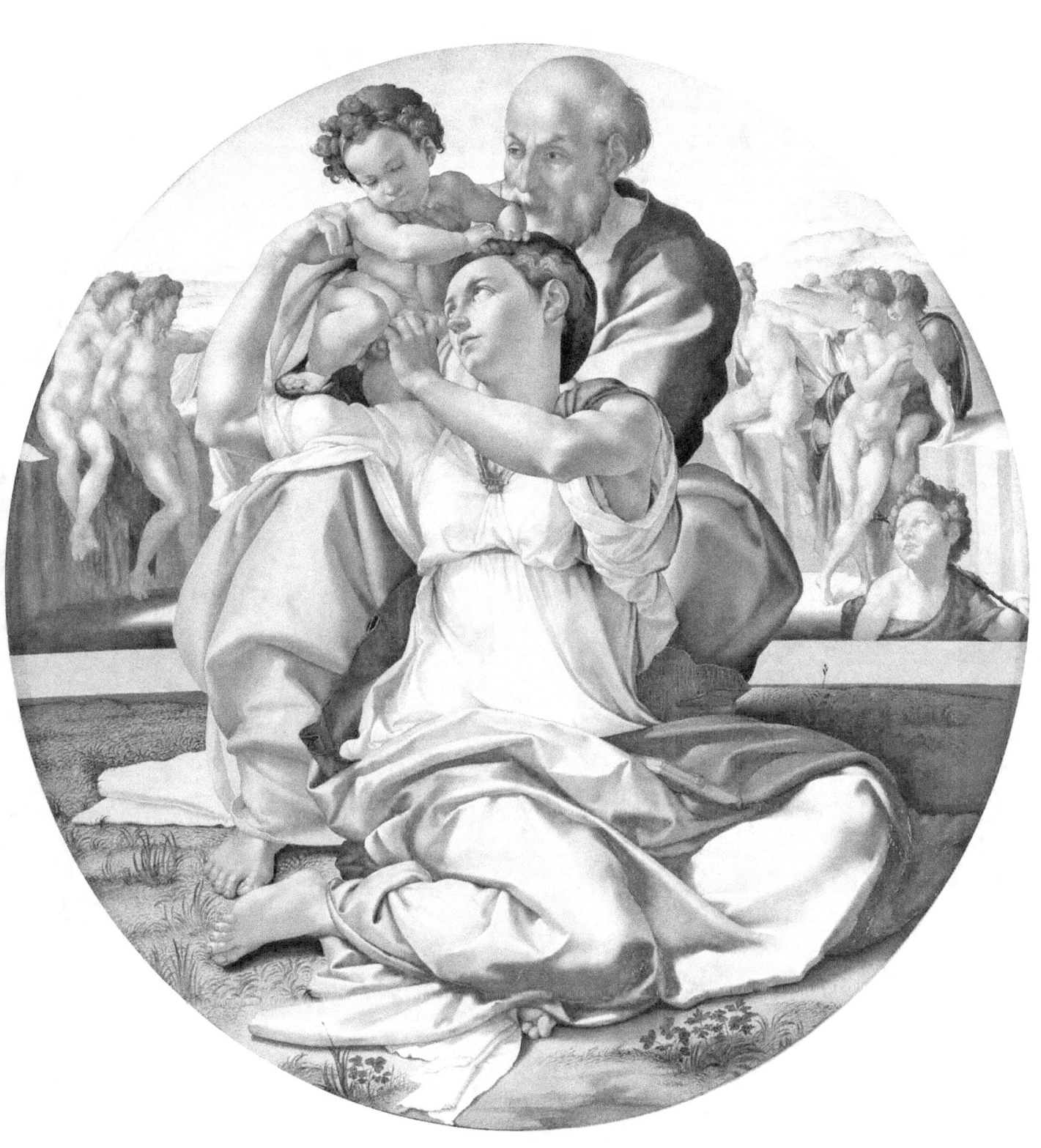

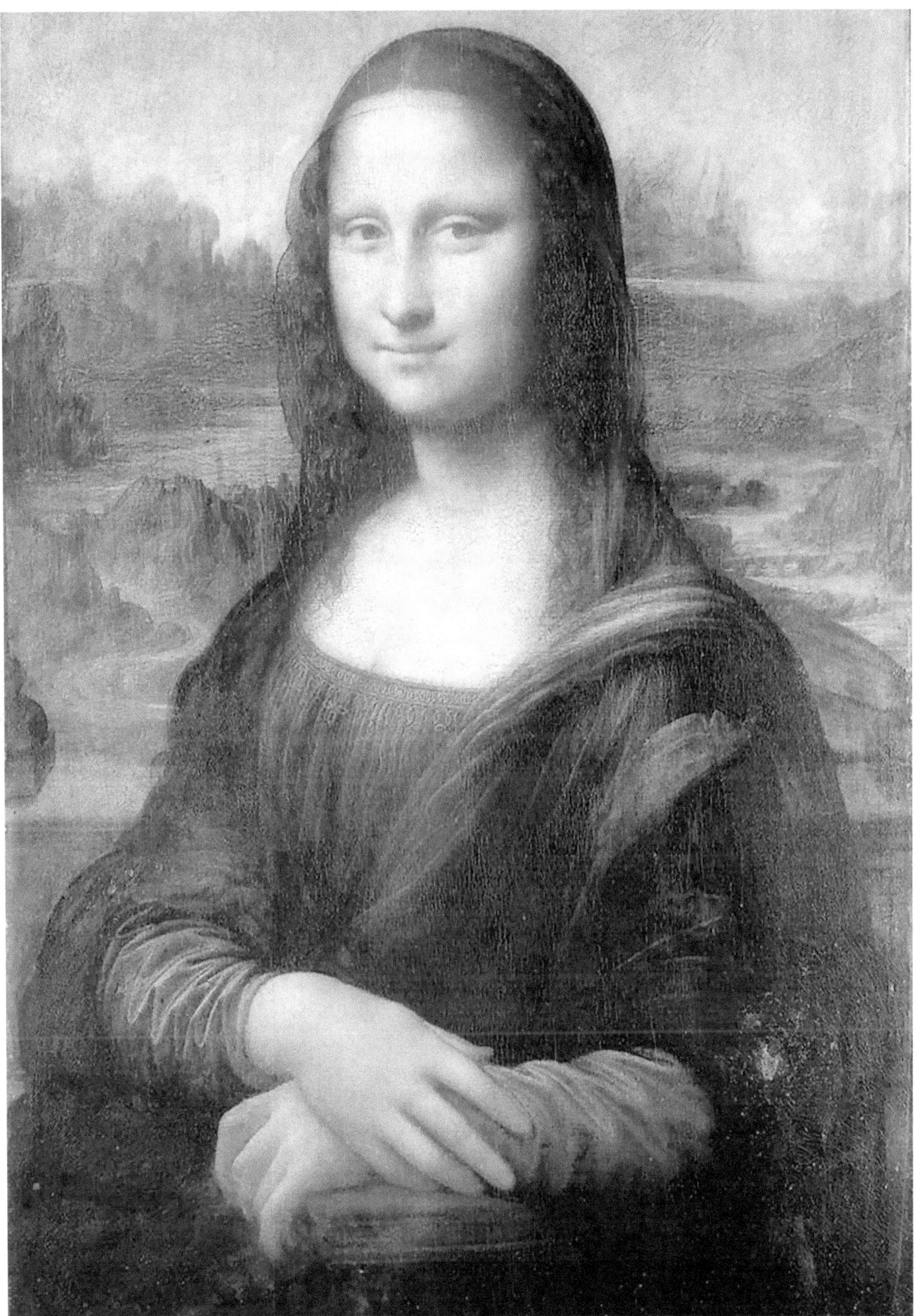

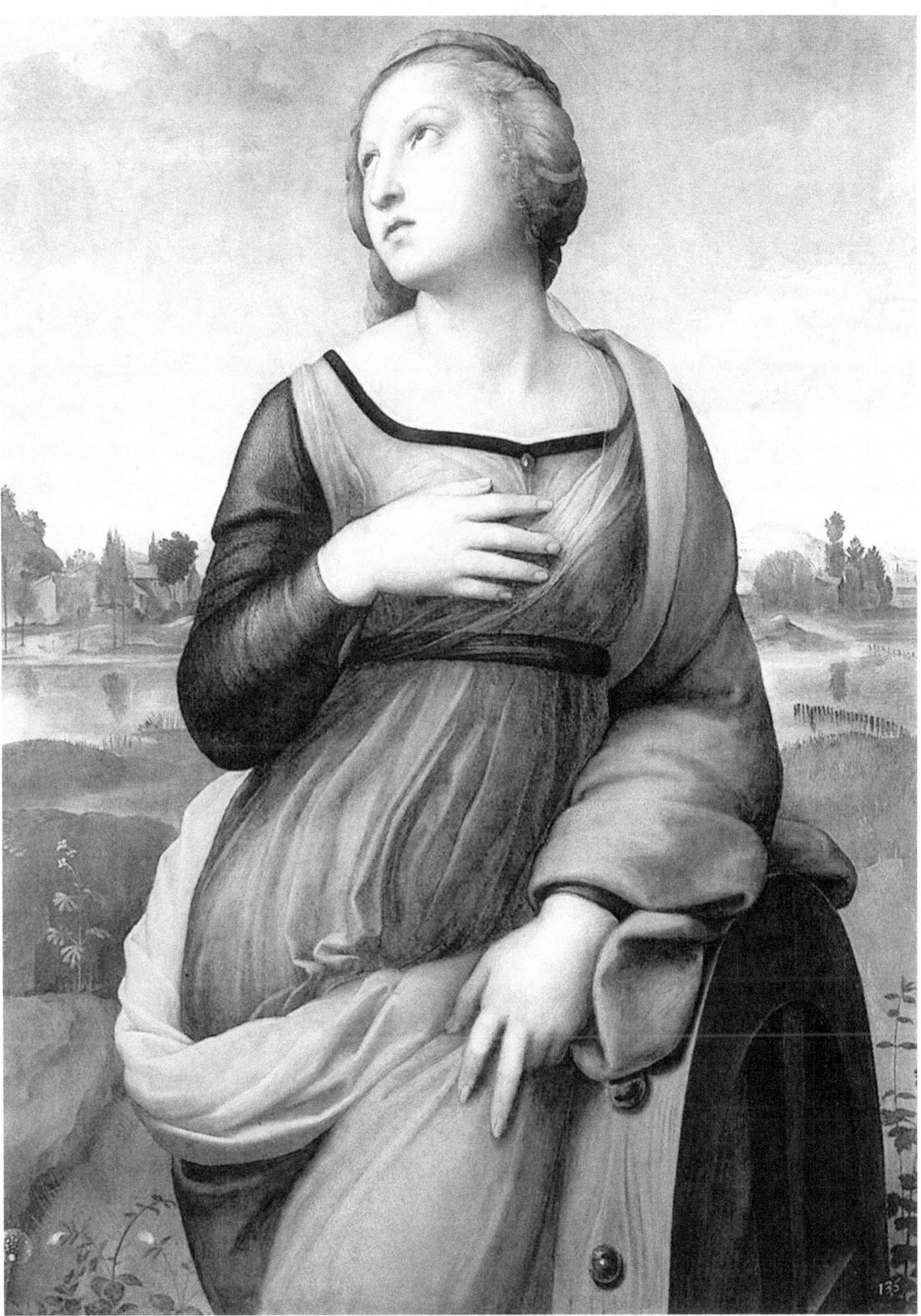

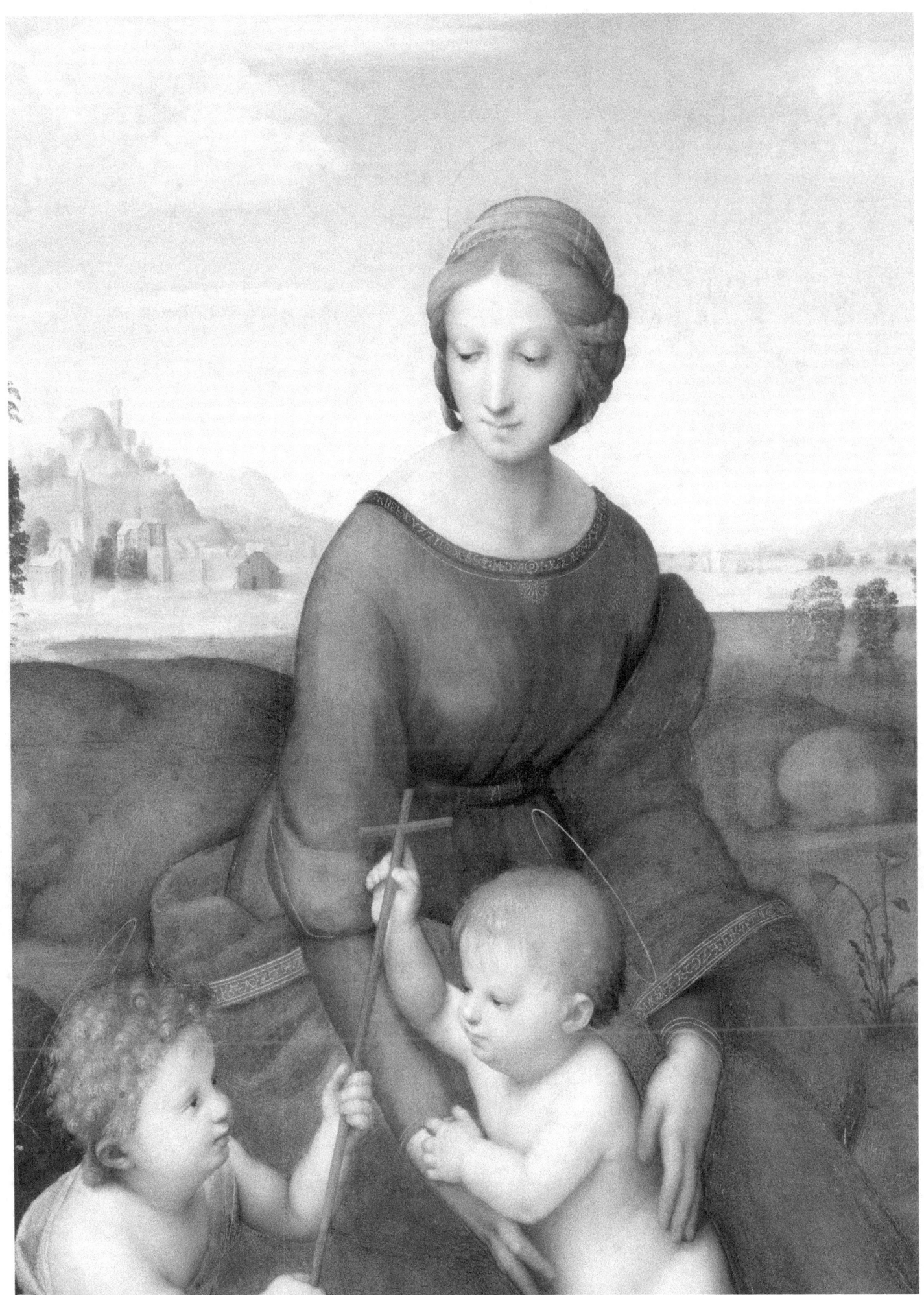

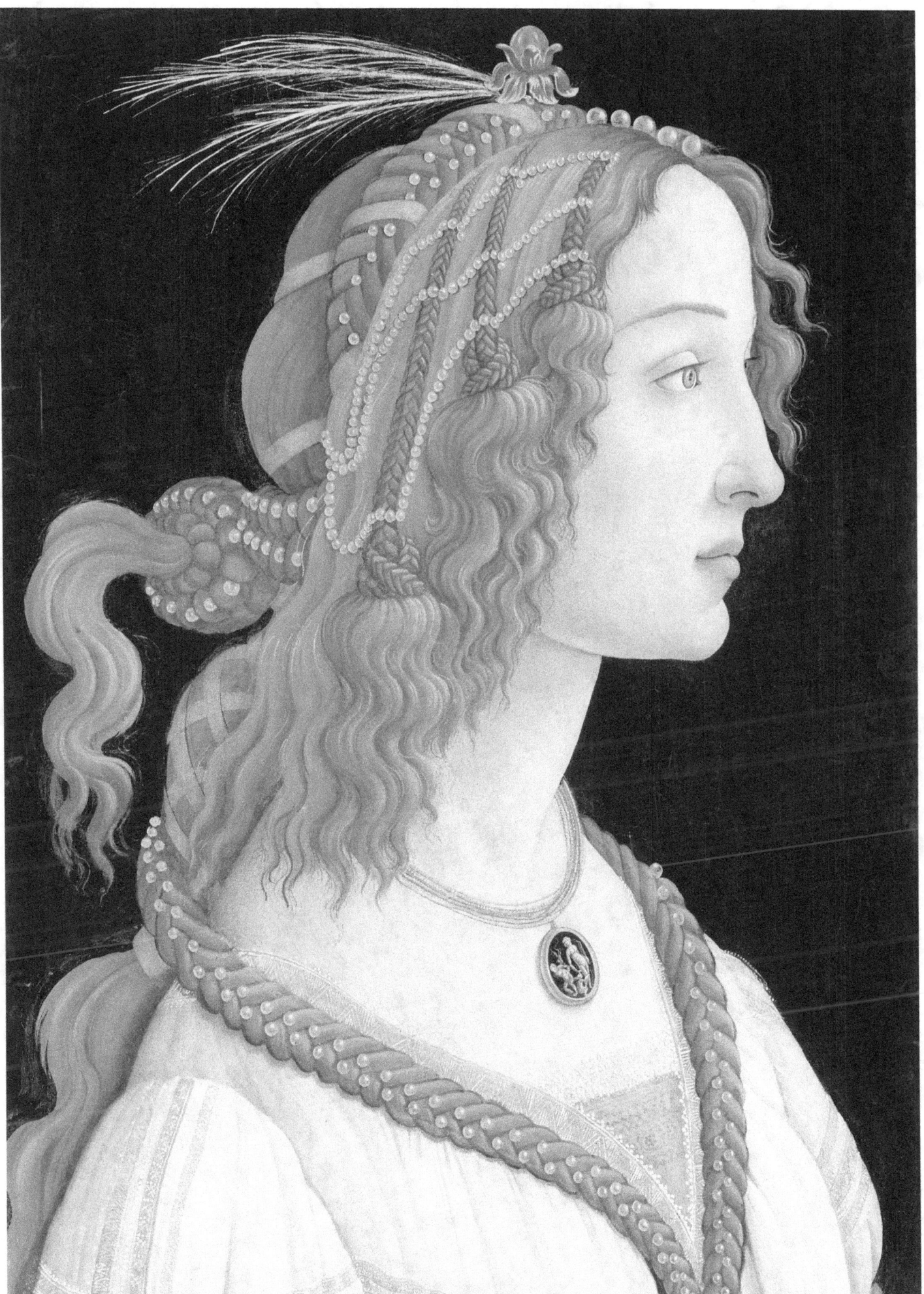

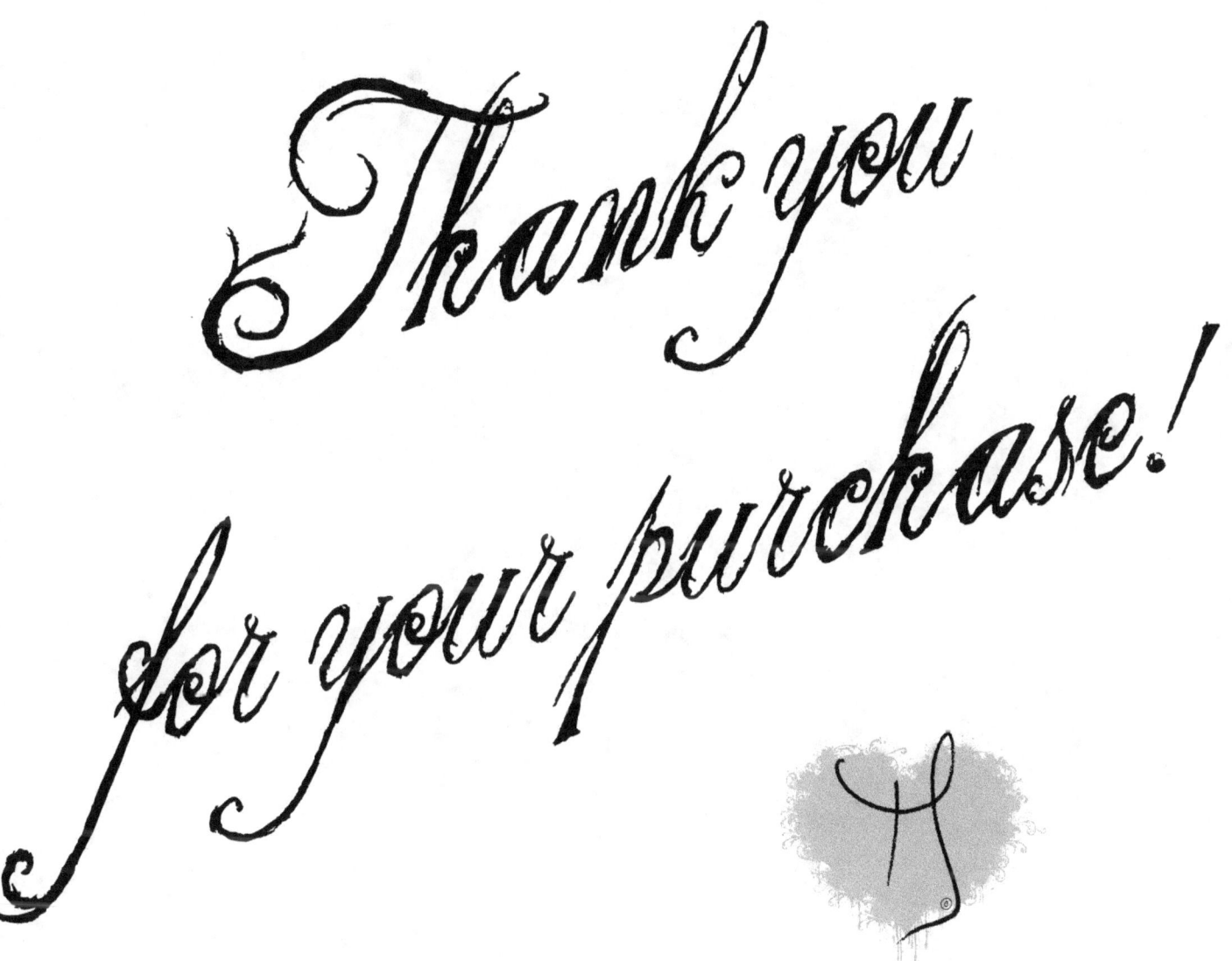

Thank you for your purchase!

To see the full catalog of my art, don't forget
to stop by
www.gothictoggs.net